FINDING CLARITY
IN A MESSY WORLD

12 SIMPLE RULES TO HELP YOU NAVIGATE
THROUGH A CONSTANT WORLD OF CHAOS

K. ARISS

ISBN: 9798377266877

Acknowledgements

To my family - You have supported me throughout my journey, and you have stuck by me through thick and thin.

To my mother – you have been my mentor, role model, and my source of strength. I owe everything to you.

To my father – you have been my biggest motivator and supporter for as long as I can remember. You never stopped believing in me, and always reminded me to believe in myself. For that, I am forever grateful.

To my sisters and brother – you are my best friends and my constant clarity in this messy world. I love you with all my heart.

To my friends who have been a part of my journey – you have inspired me, supported me, and loved me for who I am. You know who you are.

I dedicate this book to every single one of you.

K. ARISS

Table of Contents

Introduction

We live in a messy world. And it is only getting messier. We are losing our sense of direction and our sense of right and wrong. We are lost, confused, and more unfulfilled than ever. Stress levels are at an all-time global high. The rate of depression is increasing, mainly among the younger generation, and the rate of suicide is at the highest it has ever been. Society is polarized, and we are more divided. People are judging one another based on race, ethnicity, religion, skin color, gender, and even health choices. We are dealing with so much externally that we no longer have the mental capacity or energy to deal with ourselves internally. The outside chaos is fueling our inner chaos, and this needs to end. We need to find our way back to ourselves—to who we are, what drives us, and how we want to live our lives. Only then will we be able to truly find clarity in this messy, messy world.

Human beings all want the same thing. They want safety, security, connection, love, and validation. It is as simple as that. However, there is a paradoxical shift in this day and age. Our views of love, relationships, happiness, success, and identity are distorted. We no longer know how to feel or how to act. In a generation that is so used to "ghosting" instead of communicating, texting instead of calling, and cheating instead of confronting, we are more disconnected than ever. Where vulnerability was once seen as a strength, it is now viewed as attention-seeking. Where loyalty was once seen as an essential value for a successful and healthy relationship, it is now seen as stupidity. Where humility was once seen as the trait of a good human being, it is now seen as weakness.

Negative news, together with polar opposite views, cyberbullying, and hateful comments, is creating a division in society. Throw in wars, a pandemic, inflation, high living costs, and climate change, and you end up with a population on the verge of a mental breakdown.

When we are not thinking and stressing, we are on our smartphones, scrolling through social media and feeding our subconscious mind with garbage. Then stressing some more. We have forgotten how to live, how to build connections, and how to socialize. We have forgotten how to enjoy a simple moment—a place, a meal, our loved ones—without using our phones to take a photo with the sole purpose of likes. Even when we are in the elevator with someone, we take out our phones to avoid looking that person in the eye, or to avoid the awkward silence. But we keep forgetting that connections are built in exactly those moments. When we are forced to interact. To simply smile or say hello. The one device that was created to bring us closer together is drifting us further apart.

So how do we control this? How do we find clarity amid all the noise? How do we go back to the essence of what makes us human?

I have asked myself these questions for years. I have lost myself, found myself again, and been on a constant search for clarity. Coming from a multicultural background and having lived in many places throughout my childhood and adult life, I was always searching for answers, mainly within myself. As a deep thinker, I was constantly questioning everything around me. I always felt that I did not belong and that what was happening in the world was too confusing to comprehend. I would always convince myself that the grass was greener on the other side, and every time I moved somewhere new, I realized it wasn't. So I poured my heart and soul into my work wherever I went, and that became my identity. But by letting my work define me, I ended up losing who I am. I was stuck in a corporate rat race and couldn't get out. All I knew was that I was unfulfilled and unhappy. I needed to simplify the chaos that existed inside my mind, and I needed to find my purpose. So I started observing, listening, experiencing, and writing.

Through these learnings, I came to one simple conclusion. I realized that humans need discipline. They need guidance. And the way the world is currently operating is the complete opposite of that. We have unlimited choices, too much freedom, and a lot of confusion. We are losing our sense of connection. We are losing our humanity. It is more important now than ever to be able to shift through the noise.

To find clarity in this constant world of chaos, we need to take a step back. We need to go back to basics. To what makes us human.

As someone who is good at taking complex problems and simplifying them, I felt like I needed to create a blueprint or guidance for how I should live my life, and to help others do the same. A set of rules that can always help keep me in check and which I can always refer back to for reassurance that I am on the right track.

The rules provided in this book are meant to take you from Point A to Point B. They are meant to tell a story. They are logical, structured, and have a certain process to them. In order to truly find clarity, you need to apply these rules as much as you can in your lives. We will never be able to directly stop what is happening externally. What we can do, however, is influence ourselves and how we respond to things internally. This book will guide you to do just that. It will help you live your life from the inside out, and not vice versa. It will help you peel the layers of who you think you are to get to the core of who you truly are.

By sharing my main learnings and takeaways from life, I am hoping that you feel less alone, validated, and heard. Through a specific yet simple set of rules, *I want to share with you my own personal guide for finding clarity in a messy world,* and hope that you find yourself in some of my pages and words.

PART I

Rule 1:
Minimize Distractions

Shift through the noise.

→ *Minimize distractions so you are able to think clearly.*

This first rule lays the crucial foundation on which the rest of the rules are built. Currently, the external noise is dominating and not allowing us to think clearly. It is clouding our judgment. To find clarity, we need to allow our inner world to dominate. We need to live from the inside out.

Focus

If you asked someone what the three most important assets in life are, they would probably say money, time, and health. These are all true. However, there is one extremely important asset that is not talked about enough. An asset that is more applicable to the world we live in today than ever. ***Focus.*** Focus is the one thing that cannot be divided. Yet the world is trying its hardest to do just that.

We live in an era of globalization. This essentially means that the world is more interconnected today than it has ever been before. Technology is advancing at the speed of light, providing us with easy access to anything and everything. The access we have to information creates an overload, which leaves us feeling drained, overwhelmed, and confused.

The result? Disconnection.

In order to be able to focus, we need to redirect our energy to what's truly important. To do this, we need to get rid of all the unnecessary noise.

Train yourself to do more with less, and to live contently with less.

The first step is identifying anything that is in excess in your life, and either eliminating it, or decreasing it. There is a difference between needing something and wanting something. Finding that balance between wants and needs is crucial. Make a list of your daily habits. If you find yourself doing one of the following, then something is off balance:

 Spending the majority of your time on your phone or scrolling through social media and little to no time going out for walks every day or doing something productive.

 Spending too much money on things that you *want* but don't *need* in hopes that having more will make you feel more.

 Spending too much time with people that drain your energy, and less time with yourself or with people who fill you up.

There needs to be harmony between your inner world and outer world; if there isn't, then there is too much background noise. You need to turn down the volume.

The older you get, the greater need you feel to protect your peace. You realize the value of sitting cuddled up at home, eating snacks, watching a nice movie, and minding your own business. Yes, it can get lonely, but it is *peaceful*. And peace should always be chosen over unnecessary company.

True peace lies not in what you add to your life, but in what you omit. As my mom perfectly said, "If you are not occupying a certain space, you can live without it." As humans, we need the basics to survive and to be comfortable. Adding more material things to our lives will not make us more content; in fact, it will make us more confused. Having five extra bedrooms will not change the fact that we only need one bed to sleep in. Having an extra kitchen will not change the fact that we only need one place to cook and eat a nice meal. Having options is nice, but I can almost guarantee you that you will end up sticking to one room or one seat on the couch where you feel the most comfortable. In fact, having more means one extra thing to worry about, whether that is cleaning, expenses, security, or maintenance.

Similarly, if your dream is to own a yacht, how many times throughout the year will you actually have time to use it? How much will it cost you to operate and maintain it? What about taxes, insurance, and yearly harbor fees? The same goes for owning multiple cars. Aside from the expenses of insurance, maintenance, fuel costs, cleaning, and general car duties, if you own ten cars—will this make a huge difference in your life?

If you have ever been on vacation and stayed at an all-inclusive resort, you will remember that there was an availability of food options all day, every day. However, if you really think hard, how much of that food did you actually eat? You only have one stomach, and there is a certain quantity that can fit in your stomach at once. When you try to eat too much, you get stomach pain the next day. Taking too much of anything will harm you—whether it is food, drinks, or even vitamins. The same can be applied to thoughts. Thinking too much about something can cause you stress (or even a headache!).

In a world that is doing its best, day in and day out, to convince us that having more will make us feel more, doing the complete opposite is exactly what we need to do. Options create confusion. This is why the wealthiest countries in the world have the highest rates of suicide, depression, anxiety, and physical pain. Sometimes, the lack of something is what will bring us the most peace and clarity. Not having enough money will make us more focused on working hard to earn more, if that is the ultimate goal. Not owning a house will make you focused on getting *a* house, no matter how small. The lack of something provides us with a sense of direction, a goal, and the motivation to work toward that goal. It gives us something to look forward to. Today, people have too much of everything and they become depressed. They compete with a false image of "success" on social media, and it leaves them feeling empty and drained.

Social Media

Anyone who knows me knows I am not a fan of social media. And I have been very good at staying away from it over the years. That has been my therapy. I am not saying it is completely bad, because nothing is ever completely good or completely bad, but it can be very toxic if used incorrectly. And the way it has been built is setting us up for self-destruction.

There is a direct link between the use of social media and stress, depression, low self-esteem, loneliness, and anxiety. With over 59% of the global population and 90% of all young people using social media, these platforms, which include Facebook, Instagram, and Twitter, have rapidly become a central part of people's lives.[1]

It is important to note that when it comes to social media, it is not one single effect—there are many layers to it. In order to truly understand the total effect of social media in today's society, we need to look at it from a holistic perspective.

Social media, if used correctly, can be a very powerful tool. Social media democratizes information. It brings people together. It helps you connect with long-lost family members or friends from high school or college. It makes you feel like part of a community. It helps spread awareness. It helps you brand yourself and creates opportunities. For a lot of people, social media is their livelihood. It is how they promote their business or get their primary income. These include influencers, travel bloggers, authors, or entrepreneurs who market their products and services virtually.

Like many others with friends and family in different parts of the world, I know the value of connecting and staying in touch. And social media has definitely helped with that. However, at the same time, it has caused problems. It has caused misunderstandings. It has caused jealousy. It has caused disconnections. I cannot remember the last time I spoke to my cousin on the phone. Or the last time my friend from college looked me in the eyes and asked me how I was doing. Everything is either through voice notes, WhatsApp messages, DMs, or stories posted on Instagram. There is no *need* to ask anyone anything because people are sharing details about their lives *freely and willingly*.

Unconsciously, this creates a lack of effort and less value to what is being shared because what you are sharing suddenly becomes less personal and more accessible for the entire world to see.

Not only is the value lost, but people are now comparing their lives to the "fake" lives that people want you to see. Comparison is damaging generations, creating unrealistic expectations, and promoting ingratitude.

Studies also show a link between social media use and low self-esteem in both teenagers and adults. For kids and teenagers, the "perfect" pictures of other people's faces, bodies, and lives—which are enhanced by filters and editing—result in them viewing themselves and their own lives negatively, and leads to depression and insecurities. It sets false beauty standards. They start to believe that they need to look a certain way to "fit in," and this cannot be less than perfect. So what ends up happening is that people start feeling the need to prove something to those around them and continuously keep up with the latest fashion and beauty trends in order to stay current. It is almost as if social media is validating one's existence.

One important aspect is how social media and technology deliver news and information to us. Our way of receiving information has changed. We cannot tell real news from fake news, which causes stress and confusion.

If we look at what is happening in society, we will notice that people are now creating problems where there are no real problems. We are arguing about topics like gender, vaccines, and religion. This need for struggle in our lives, coupled with a lack of focus and direction, is causing us to say things and be involved in debates and discussions that are simply wasting our time and stressing us out.

Social media provides a platform for people to be negative, hateful, and to complain, while hiding behind their anonymity. It allows them to finally have a voice without having to show who they are and without the accountability that comes with their words. These are the people we hear from the most. On the other hand, the "doers" are just doing and not spending time trying to show or prove it. What ends up happening is that people eventually start to believe the complainers, and the doers are now the ones who feel like they have lost their voice.

Solution

In order to navigate through an era of social media, we need to understand it and find its antidote. The problem is not in social media; it is in how we are using it. By understanding social media and how it works, we can understand ourselves better and create the discipline to control it rather than it controlling us. The key here is *balance*.

When something is in excess, it throws your body off balance. Remember, the first step is identifying all the things in your life that are in excess, and eliminating them, or decreasing them.

Firstly, we need to understand how social media works. It is all controlled through algorithms. These algorithms are developed to tailor specific content to specific individuals based on their interests. They detect mood, behavior, and patterns, and deliver content accordingly. What ends up happening is that you hit "like" or spend time on a specific post, ad or video, which triggers the algorithm to keep sending you more of that content. If you are focusing on motivational, positive and uplifting posts, then that's a good thing. You will keep receiving more of that. However, if you are sad, depressed, or going through a heartbreak or the loss of a loved one, chances are you will get even more upset by being on your phone. If you are following models, influencers, or people who appear to have a "better" life than you, you are going to keep comparing yourself to them and end up getting more depressed.

Then there is the effect of dopamine. The dopamine hit we get from the alerts, "likes," and comments on social media makes it very difficult to control our usage. Just like a drug. The dopamine hit can be highly addictive, regardless of the intended use of social media. With every new picture we upload, we start comparing the number of likes with the number we got on our last picture and find that with each hit, we need to increase the dose to get that same pleasure or instant gratification. So, what ends up happening is an "all or nothing" effect. We either stay away from it completely or surrender to the addiction.

So what are some practical steps you can take?

If you are a business owner and can afford to, hire someone to take care of the digital marketing. If you are an influencer, make sure that social media does not consume you and that you are in control of it—not the other way around. This is easier said than done. But if there is a will, there is a way. Start small. Try to find minor ways to limit your intake of the dopamine hit. This can include training yourself to wake up in the morning and not look at your phone, sleeping with your phone in another room or on "airplane mode," or simply spending one less hour of scroll time each day. These solutions require a tremendous amount of self-discipline, but they are highly beneficial in the long run. Avoid watching the news, listening to politics, and reading negative comments. It will change your life. What you give your energy to, grows.

Mindfulness – The Gift of the Present

Another essential thing you can do is to practice mindfulness. Mindfulness is the human ability to be fully present and aware of what we are doing in a specific moment. It is such a basic concept, but it is drifting further and further away each day.

Ask yourself one question. If someone fell on the floor or if you saw two people physically fighting, how many people (including yourself) would actually run up to the person and help them? And how many would take out their phones to take a photo or video to post online? People are so focused on chasing the likes that their sole focus becomes on capturing the moment instead of living it. We need to remind ourselves to take a step back, breathe, and reconnect with ourselves and with those around us by disconnecting from technology.

Be intentional. Before taking out your phone to take a photo of someone or something, ask yourself why you are doing it. Ask yourself what you are hoping to achieve by posting it online for the world to see. Most importantly, ask yourself if it is worth it. Instead, take a mental picture in your mind and truly experience and live the moment. Believe me; it will last much longer than a photo on your phone.

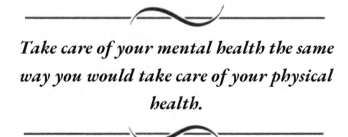

Take care of your mental health the same way you would take care of your physical health.

KEY TAKEAWAYS

The first step in finding clarity is by shifting through the noise. This is done in several ways:

1. Make a list of your daily habits—do this every day.

2. Notice the toxic patterns and set intentional goals to break them.

3. Once you set a goal—be disciplined.

4. Be still and minimize distractions. Only then will you be able to think clearly.

5. Be careful what you feed your mind—stay away from garbage.

6. Eliminate unnecessary noise. This can be through simply walking in nature without any form of technology and listening to the quiet.

7. Learn to detach from your phone (overcome separation anxiety).

8. Disconnect from technology in order to connect.

9. Guard and protect your energy—*your inner peace.*

Rule 2:
Understand Yourself.
Self-awareness is Key

Practice self-awareness

→ *Work on understanding your inner chaos so you can navigate through the outer chaos.*

Once you have turned down the noise, you can begin to listen. To apply this next rule correctly, we must first go back to the basics and understand how we think, what drives us, and what beliefs shape us. Our mental state is a direct representation of how we see the world. By quieting down our inner chaos, we can learn to navigate through the outer chaos.

The first question we need to ask ourselves is: Do we understand what is going on inside our minds enough to understand ourselves?

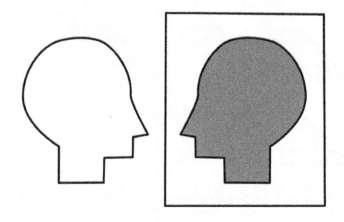

First, look at your relationship with yourself—what is your own self-image and self-worth? Start with you. Having a solid starting point and being in a good place with yourself and within yourself is crucial, because it will determine your ability to cope with the world.

When you look in the mirror—what do you see?

Core Beliefs

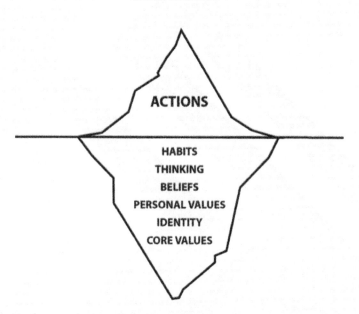

We all know that our childhood plays a very important role in shaping who we are today. As depicted by the Iceberg Model, our actions and behaviors are dictated by our values, beliefs, thoughts, and identity, which were formed during our childhood. These thoughts, values, and beliefs are at the core of who we are and are not visible on the outside. The way in which they manifest themselves is through behavior, and this is ultimately what we see.

So what exactly are beliefs, and how is all of this linked together?

Our thoughts form our beliefs, which in turn, dictate our actions. Beliefs are assumptions we make about the world, and our values stem from those beliefs.

Let's go a bit deeper. A thought that is repeated very often and assumed to be true becomes a belief. We usually have the same thoughts every day, which means that over time, we end up developing a habit of thinking a certain way. Habits are routines of behavior that are repeated regularly and tend to occur subconsciously.

Core beliefs are our most deeply embedded assumptions about ourselves and the world around us, which we believe to be true. They shape our worldview and self-image. Our core beliefs are developed in early childhood and are a result of our upbringing and experiences.

Think of core beliefs like a pair of sunglasses. Everyone has a different lens that causes them to see things differently. For many people, these core beliefs are negative and cause them to view themselves and the world negatively, resulting in negative consequences.

Here are some examples:

I'm unlovable	I'm stupid	I'm boring
I'm not good enough	I'm ugly	I'm worthless
I'm a bad person	I'm difficult	I'm undeserving

By the age of seven, most of our behavioral patterns, core beliefs, and habits are developed, and this carries on subconsciously throughout our adult life. In order to understand why that happens, we must first understand the human brain.

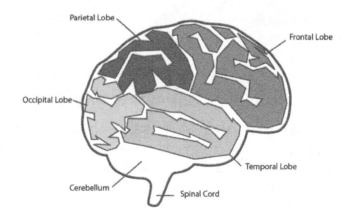

Parietal Lobe

Frontal Lobe

Occipital Lobe

Temporal Lobe

Cerebellum

Spinal Cord

The brain can be divided into several parts. In simplified terms, the frontal lobe is the conscious part of our brain—our Highest Self. This part is calm, rational, and wise. The limbic system is the part of the brain that is involved in our behavioral and emotional responses. This is sometimes referred to as the "emotional machine" or our "gremlins." We can also consider it our inner child. This part is emotional, irrational, and responsible for making us feel things that we do not always want to feel and behave in ways that are beyond our control. Although they are two separate systems, the power play between them is crucial and determines our behaviors and how we see the world. Throughout the brain, we also have a software or tape recorder that takes input from all our different parts and stores them. This information is then used to act automatically. This software is programmed early on and serves as our subconscious mind.

The goal is to reach and operate from our Highest Self—the one that is conscious and calls the shots. The one that has all the other parts under control.

What separates us from almost all of the animal kingdom is the front part of the brain—the frontal lobe. It operates at a brain wavelength of alpha or beta and gets switched on only by the age of seven. Before that, the brain operates in delta or theta wavelengths without any critical thinking. This means that up until the age of seven, our conscious brain is still not activated. We are like sponges, absorbing every single thing from our surroundings. What our parents tell us, we take to be the truth. How our parents behave, we model. How our parents view us, is how we view ourselves. Our habits and beliefs are formed subconsciously from a young age, which makes us very impressionable as children.

"Give me the child for seven years, and I'll give you the man."

– Aristotle

Our childhood years, sub-seven, is also when our opinion of ourselves is formed. This sticks with us throughout adulthood and explains why people usually never rise above the opinion of themselves. We see ourselves through the eyes of our parents, and it becomes very difficult to change that view. If our parents tell us from a young age that we are difficult, we grow up thinking we are difficult. If they tell us we are lazy, we grow up thinking we are lazy. If they tell us we are strong, beautiful, and special, we grow up believing all those things. Our parents teach us how to love ourselves long before we know who we are, or what love even means.

As we grow older and start to have our own experiences outside our homes, we begin to be conscious about things in our surroundings. We start to care a bit more about what our friends think, and less about what our parents think. But through it all, our core beliefs are in the driver's seat, even if we don't realize it. This carries on with us until adulthood and becomes the lens through which we see the world. When it comes to relationships, we end up accepting the love we think we deserve.

A few weeks ago, I was in the car with my three-year-old nephew, Adam. We were both sitting in the backseat, and he had a bottle of water. As he was drinking, the car came to a sudden stop, and he spilled water on his clothes and mine. His initial reaction was frustration, and I could tell he was about to get upset. At the same moment, I pointed at my wet sleeves and said, "Oh no, look, Adam! I got water all over my clothes." In that instant, he suddenly forgot about himself and his own clothes, and looked at me and said, "It's okay, auntie. It's okay, it will dry." Instead of being reactive, his subconscious programming kicked in, and his automatic behavior was to reassure me that it was okay—the same way that his mother reassures him whenever something similar happens to him. It was the emotional response of me getting upset that triggered his behavior.

This was very interesting. I compared it to another situation I had witnessed at the airport in London just one month prior. A child was carrying a Duty-Free bag for his stressed mother, and they were frantically running to the gate of their flight. Suddenly, the child accidentally dropped the bag on the floor, and the glass inside shattered. His mother, who was ahead of him, turned around and furiously said to him, "Tom! Look at what you've done! That was an expensive bottle of wine!" She was screaming at him in the middle of the airport in front of everyone. The child looked at her with sad eyes and did not say a single word. It was clear that he did not mean to drop the bag. It was an accident. He made a mistake. Even though she was stressed and probably reacted in the heat of the moment, that boy took it very hard on himself. The emotional response of his mother getting angry probably caused his subconscious mind to tell him that he was stupid, or that he was a difficult boy.

It is important to note here that we should by no means judge anyone in any situation because we are all doing our best, but it is important to understand how the mind works so we can be more mindful when it comes to the words we choose to say and how we choose to say them.

Our core beliefs are at the center of who we are. If we believe that we are difficult or unworthy, we usually start to form associations with those beliefs. Difficult equals bad. Unworthy equals unlovable. Curious equals rebellious. Our fears are then based on those beliefs and associations. We might have a fear of ending up alone because we believe wc are difficult, and therefore, we are bad or difficult to love. This also forms our needs, which in this case, is the need to be loved. We develop defense mechanisms that protect us from those fears. We can sabotage good relationships or be drawn to toxic ones. Our behaviors will present themselves in different ways, depending on several factors, both internal and external.

So, we now know that the core beliefs we developed as children have little to do with us, and mostly to do with our environment. We were being programmed using the words that were spoken to us, especially by our caretakers, and which we took to be true.

So, how do we heal?

Behaviors

To begin challenging our negative core beliefs, we must first recognize what they are. Core beliefs are ultimately what you want to identify to truly have a starting point to heal. It is not always easy to know what our core beliefs are, because they can be deeply rooted. Self-awareness is key. The first step in understanding your core beliefs is by identifying your behavioral patterns. Look for those patterns in your life. Whether it is the type of people you attract, the type of relationships you go into, whom you spend your time with, or even how you spend money. Pay very close attention to those patterns. They will tell you where you need to heal. Once we identify those patterns, we can identify habits. Then we can recognize behaviors, and then thought processes. Once we have identified that, we can identify beliefs. Working backward is the most effective way to reach the root cause of the problem.

Now, the good news. The moment we recognize our core beliefs—we *can* change them. Is it easy? No. But is it doable? Absolutely. If repeated thoughts create beliefs, then by changing our thoughts and repeating them often enough, we can replace those negative beliefs with new, positive ones. Just like the tape in a recorder. The tape itself cannot be changed, but we can record over it. This is what is done in Cognitive Behavioral Therapy (CBT).

CORE BELIEF

Suppose your core belief is that you are unworthy or unlovable. In that case, you can work with a therapist or do your own work to understand what exactly happened in your childhood or throughout your adult experiences that made you develop that belief. You can dig deep to identify and understand the thoughts you had and the truths you associated with those thoughts, which led to you developing that belief. Usually, that core belief manifests itself in attachment styles and our relationships—both personal and professional.

Example

If you tend to attract toxic people to your life, maybe you notice that you talk negatively about yourself, to yourself. By identifying this habit, you can identify the behavior, which could be that you do not treat yourself kindly, and therefore, people tend to treat you the same way. You need to ask yourself: "What is my thought process that allows me to not value myself? How do I talk to myself internally?" This leads you to identify beliefs about yourself so you can put in the work to change them.

"Your beliefs become your thoughts, your thoughts become your words, your words become your actions, your actions become your habits, your habits become your values, your values become your destiny."

- MK Gandhi

It is important to note here that most of the work can be done on your own. A therapist asks you the right questions and provides you with the tools and safe space to unravel your mind and understand yourself better, but ultimately it is you who puts in the work. Finding a therapist you connect with is key because no matter what they say to you, you will not make any progress if you do not feel comfortable and understood by them. In fact, it might have the opposite effect.

Thoughts

An essential step to changing our core beliefs is by managing our thoughts. Our thoughts control how we feel about ourselves and the world around us. Positive thoughts make us feel good and negative thoughts can put us down. Remember, a repeated thought that we assume to be true becomes a belief.

Our negative thoughts are often irrational and can result in depression, poor self-esteem, and anxiety. You can be someone who frequently receives positive feedback at work, but one single criticism can make you feel like you are terrible at your job. Your irrational thoughts about your performance at work can control how you feel about yourself and, ultimately, how you view yourself.

In order to get rid of your negative thoughts, you need to look at things holistically. Instead of thinking you are not good at this job because of one single mistake, look at all the good things you have done in the past at work. Look at all the things you have done right instead of the things you have done wrong. Focus on your skills, your strengths, and why they hired you for this position in the first placc. You got this job because you were the best suited and most qualified for this job. Own that, trust that, and believe that.

By identifying our negative thoughts, challenging them, and replacing them with new rational thoughts, we can change how we feel.

Trigger	Negative Thought	New Thought
Example: I made a mistake at work	"I'm going to get fired. I always mess up. I'm not good enough."	"I messed up, but mistakes happen. I'm going to work through this, like I always do."

Let's do a little exercise:

How is your relationship with yourself?

What do you tell yourself when you look in the mirror?

What are some of your negative thoughts (about yourself and the world)?

Is there substantial evidence for those thoughts?

Is there evidence contrary to your thoughts?

What is a situation that happened recently that triggered a negative thought?

What would a friend think about this situation?

Will this matter a year from now? How about five years from now?

What are some patterns in your life?

What is one of your negative core beliefs?

List three pieces of evidence contrary to your negative core belief:

1. _____

2. _____

3. _____

Now that we have identified some of our thoughts and core beliefs, the next step is to look at how they manifest themselves in our adult life and lead to ineffective behavioral patterns. Some of those examples are listed below:

Insecurity

- You are uncomfortable in your own skin and feel very insecure about yourself. This manifests itself in both your personal and professional life.

- You don't feel attractive enough and keep asking yourself why anyone would want to be with you.

- At work, you constantly try to please your boss and colleagues by saying yes to unnecessary meetings and tasks, and working extra hours.

- Low self-esteem prevents you from setting boundaries with people you know are not good for you. You don't want to let go of the person who once acccpted you for who you are because you feel like no one will ever accept you again.

- Even though you are unhappy in the relationship and are not being treated right, you feel like you will not find anyone better than the person you're with, so you stay with them. You accept the love you think you deserve.

- You find yourself doubting your intuition a lot. You do not trust yourself, and therefore, you find it difficult to follow what feels right. So even if you feel like you should leave, you will keep going back to the toxic relationship.

Self-doubt

- You have such extreme clarity, experience, and wisdom, but the one thing that keeps getting in the way over and over and over again, is doubt.

- What keeps getting you in trouble is not the decision you make about something or someone, but the decisions you end up making *after* that initial decision. And that second time is driven by regret, which in turn, is driven by doubt. This is why you keep revisiting the past, over and over again, even though, in that specific moment, your gut told you that this was the right thing to do.

Fear

- The one thing that is greater than our needs is our fear. We can have a need for trust, but our fear of letting someone in and getting betrayed prevents us from opening up.

- Although you know deep down that you deserve better, the fear of not finding someone better and ending up alone overcomes your need to be loved right.

- The fear of not finding another job causes you to stay in the same job and be miserable.

- The fear of failure prevents you from putting yourself out there and trying something new.

- The fear of rejection prevents you from asking that person out or applying for that job you want.

Shame

- Although you may not have done anything wrong, you are ashamed of *who* you are. Unhealed wounds cause you to suffer inwardly.

- Shame can also be the result of something that happened to you. This can be due to childhood trauma that you may or may not remember.

- If you have ever been in a toxic relationship and/or the victim of abuse, you can feel ashamed of allowing yourself to be used and abused in that way. That shame is what kept you silent at the time, and what is keeping you silent today. You feel like you cannot talk to anyone because no one will understand. You suffer silently.

- This leads to a loss of self-esteem over time and can also lead to addiction, depression, self-harm, and violence.

- You need to remember that what happened to you was **not** your fault and that you acted with the knowledge and experience you had at the time.

Guilt

- Guilt is the feeling of remorse after we have done something and it stems from our actions. Although it is usually linked to how we affect those around us, in reality, guilt has very little to do with how we affect others and more to do with how it makes us feel about ourselves.

- The feeling of guilt is linked to our values, which in turn, stem from our core beliefs. Too much guilt can lead to shame.

- You may have a substance addiction, which causes you to lie, manipulate, and behave in ways that are irrational. Your actions hurt those around you, especially those you deeply care about. This leads to you feeling guilty for hurting or upsetting them. More importantly, it is the act of going against your values that makes you feel that guilt.

- You were betrayed by your partner or close friend. Even though that person hurt and betrayed you, you feel guilty for walking away and choosing yourself.

- You are someone who is constantly there for others and always puts their needs above your own. The one time you felt you needed a break and put yourself first, you felt guilty.

- Although you did not hurt anyone, your core beliefs made you feel like putting yourself first makes you a bad or selfish person.

RESULTING BEHAVIORAL PATTERN

Everything is interlinked. If we believe we are unlovable, this can lead to us becoming insecure and anxious as adults. We fear ending up alone. If our core belief is that we are stupid, this can present as self-doubt as adults. If we believe we are unworthy, this will manifest as shame. If our core belief is that we are selfish and we associate that with being a bad person, then every time we prioritize ourselves, we will feel guilty. Insecurity, self-doubt, shame, and guilt will all result in destructive behavioral patterns such as self-sabotage or people-pleasing. Let's take a look at two examples of self-sabotage.

Self-sabotage

Example 1

Something inside you, deeply rooted, makes you feel like you are unworthy. There is something that makes you feel that you are not good enough. You are not lovable enough. You are not pretty enough. You are not woman/man enough. Because you don't believe that you are worthy, you don't believe people who tell you that you are. You don't believe people who tell you that they love you. Because if you don't fully love yourself, how can someone else? You are your biggest critic and your own worst enemy. Because you have no control over these things, you try to control the things you do have power over. Like money. Like your things. You are extremely possessive, to the point where you sometimes feel like you don't know how to live. You cannot let go of minor details, and you try to control every aspect of your life, up to the point of what you eat or how you dress. It causes you anxiety. You are obsessing over unnecessary things. It is not healthy. Your need for perfection is linked to your need to please others. By doing so, you end up sabotaging yourself.

Example 2

You felt a little extra lonely today, and your thoughts started taking over. They triggered emotions inside you that made you start thinking about your ex and reminiscing on the good times. Your need to be loved and your fear of ending up alone overpowered your logic. You wrote a long message to them, even though they had made it very clear that they wanted nothing to do with you. Instead of pausing and thinking, you went based on impulse and pressed send. The moment you did, you regretted it and felt extremely shitty about yourself. This resulted in you going into a cycle of self-destruction.

Inner child

We all have an inner child that never goes away. It is our job to take care of that inner child—to nurture it, care for it, and give it love and attention. When it is not being taken care of, it cries for attention in the form of tantrums, emotions, and unexplainable behavior. Identifying the triggers that cause our inner child to react is important.

Remember, we are made up of different parts that sometimes work against each other to protect us in their own way. We need to acknowledge and understand those parts so they can befriend each other and start working together to help us heal.

The most important relationship is between the parts that *protect* us from pain (our "protectors") and those child parts that are *in* pain (our "exiles").

The same situation can trigger different parts to react in different ways. The part that is *in* pain can start crying out for help in the form of triggers, emotions, and negative self-view and self-worth. The part that is trying to protect us from pain causes us to behave in ways that will never make us feel that pain again.

Truly understanding these concepts will help us not only understand our childhood, experiences, and beliefs, but it will help us be kinder to ourselves. The words that were spoken to us as kids are not the truth. They do not define us. Difficult does not mean unworthy. Curious does not mean rebellious. Rude does not mean unlovable. More importantly, wanting love, care and affection does not make us needy. Wanting a toy when our parents were struggling financially does not make us bad or unworthy kids. Our caretakers did their best given their circumstances and the knowledge they had at the time, and it is now up to us to heal ourselves and future generations with the knowledge that we currently possess.

Now that we have identified and understood the core beliefs that are dictating our self-image and behaviors, we can move on to the next part.

KEY TAKEAWAYS

- Our mental state directly affects how we see the world.

- We all just want to be understood. But we tend to forget that it is more important for us to understand ourselves first. And to do so without judgment.

- Everything we do is driven by core beliefs, which form our associations, fears, and needs.

- Core beliefs are also responsible for our insecurities, self-doubt, and need for validation and approval.

- Take the time to truly understand yourself. Don't be scared. Read, ask questions, write, seek therapy, and talk to a loved one.

- Understand that our brains are made up of different "parts." Do the work and become so self-aware that your Highest Self is in control, not your emotions.

- Start by looking at the relationship you have with yourself. What kind of self-talk do you have with yourself? Is it negative? Do you put yourself down? What are your triggers? What are your insecurities and fears?

- Next, look at the relationships you have with those around you. Are they healthy? Are they dysfunctional? How do they make you feel about yourself?

- Finally, look at your behavioral patterns. Is there a pattern or trend in the people you are attracted to and how you act?

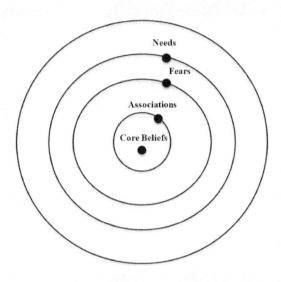

- Identify your behavioral patterns so you can identify your thought process and core beliefs.

- You need to work to reprogram the software, or record over the tape.

- **Thoughts → Emotions → Beliefs → Behaviors → Way of Living**

Rule 3:

Own Who You Are

Once you have reached a certain level of understanding yourself → Own it.

Y ou cannot own who you are if you don't understand who you are. Understanding who you are is digging deep, doing the work, and learning about the experiences that shaped your thoughts, beliefs, and behavioral patterns (Rule #2). Owning who you are is being kind, graceful, and gentle with yourself. It is loving every single part of who you were and who you are—the past and the present. It is valuing yourself and being confident with your flaws. It is embracing your imperfections and not apologizing for the mistakes you made before you understood why you were making them. It is working on who you want to become and bettering yourself each day. It is about owning the messiness, the imperfections, the flaws, and the strengths—all of it.

We all reach a point in our lives when we ask ourselves: who am I?

Knowing who we are is *hard*. The truth is, we all have an ongoing battle inside of us, and we are all struggling. This is life. It is a journey. Nothing is meant to be constant; we are designed to keep having internal struggles in order to figure out who we are and what we want from this life every second of every day. Without these battles, we would not be able to better ourselves. We would not be able to understand ourselves.

In order to truly figure out who we are, we need to know who we are not. Through the process of elimination, we can get closer to understanding ourselves—what drives us, what upsets us, what makes us happy, and most importantly, *what values and beliefs shape and dictate us.*

Own your mistakes

An essential part of understanding who we are is through making mistakes. Mistakes are a healthy part of life. They give us clarity. As long as we make a mistake and learn from it, it is just that—a mistake. It will help us grow and get more in touch with who we are. However, a mistake repeated *consciously* more than once becomes a decision. Sometimes, the same mistake can present itself in different forms— that is life's way of trying to tell us something. It is life's way of telling us that there is a lesson we need to learn. Until we have identified what that lesson is, we will keep repeating that same mistake.

Your mistakes do not define you; they tell you who you're not.

Most of us are extremely hard on ourselves. We give ourselves such a hard time after we have said or done something, and we go into a negative, self-hatred spiral. We need to learn to recognize that we are only human; everything we go through is a healthy part of life that is helping us get one step closer to understanding who we are. Own your decisions. Own your words. Own your mistakes. Take accountability. The moment you do that, you no longer give power to anyone else to affect you, and you no longer surrender to feelings of regret, guilt, or shame.

We are so caught up on the minute details of who we think we are—the way we look, the way we dress, the way we speak—that we tend to overlook who we *really* are at the core. We are too afraid of going to the gym because we do not want to look ridiculous in front of all the "fit" people. We are too afraid of asking a basic question in front of our colleagues for fear of looking stupid. We are too afraid of taking on a new hobby or sport as adults because we think that adults should not learn anything new and are too old for that. We are afraid to say no to unnecessary meetings for fear of being judged. Some of us are actually afraid of speaking up in front of others and sharing our ideas and knowledge because we do not want to make others uncomfortable. We are afraid of shining too bright in their eyes, so we prefer to stay in the dark. Owning who you are is not only about owning your mistakes, but it is also about owning your strengths. It is the self-talk you have with yourself on a daily basis. It is the understanding and realization that we are all only human—we are all very different yet *very* similar—and we all have similar fears and insecurities. It is the ability to throw yourself into new situations, environments, tasks, and hobbies and have absolute faith in yourself that you will crush it. That no matter how silly you look, you are so damn *brave*. You dared to step inside the arena. You will leave feeling extremely proud of yourself for trying, for challenging yourself, and for stepping outside your comfort zone. You are stronger than you think. And every single person around you will admire you for that strength because they wish they had just a little bit of it themselves. It is extremely important to remember that when you do step outside your comfort zone and you do succeed, do not feel guilty about it. Don't let imposter syndrome take over. If you have it, good—it means that you care. But never, ever let it linger on for too long. You got to where you are because of *who* you are. Own that.

Believing and trusting in our capacity as human beings means that we do not have to fit into society's standards of what and who we should be. You can be ambitious but also humble. You can be successful but also put family first. You can have money but still search for inner peace.

You do not necessarily have to know who you are right now because it is a journey, but it is about owning who you are at this specific moment. If you are confused, own that. If you made mistakes, own that. Just whatever you do, don't put yourself down.

Don't give people more power than they deserve.

The moment you realize that you are not better than or less than anyone, you stop living to impress people. You no longer seek validation and approval from those around you because you understand and recognize that everyone is struggling, and everyone is on their own journey. You cannot please everyone, no matter how hard you try. Truly understanding this concept will not only liberate you, but it will empower you. So don't give people more power than they deserve.

People often think their value decreases based on someone's inability to see their worth. A diamond will always be a diamond, whether someone wants it or not. Some may find it too expensive and choose not to buy it—that doesn't make it any less of a diamond. Others may appreciate its beauty and believe it deserves to be bought for that price—those are the people we should look for in our lives. We should never attempt to sell ourselves to anyone because a true diamond should lay still and attract people just by being.

Stay away from people who try to antagonize your character.

Sometimes we are put in situations in life that test our character and show us who we really are at our core. I always believe that a person's true character is revealed by the choices they make when no one is watching. When they are all alone, with nothing but their thoughts, and when they have the complete freedom to say, think, and act however they want.

Character is everything, no matter how much money you have in your bank account and how many cars you own—without character, people will neither respect nor appreciate you. You can be the most attractive person in the world, but if you do not have the character to match it up, people will look past it.

If we pay close enough attention, we can see people's souls—through what they say, how they say it, and when they choose to say it. There's a line from a song by *The Script* that I absolutely love. It goes, *"Stand for something, or fall for anything."* It is extremely rare to find people who stand up for what they believe in nowadays, especially in a work or corporate setting. We are so afraid all the time—afraid of our bosses and colleagues and that we might say or do something that will make us lose our jobs. So we end up doing and saying things we don't

K. ARISS

really believe in just because it is "politically right." In turn, we lose touch with our sense of self and who we are, and it leaves us feeling drained and miserable.

Be Intentional

Owning who you are in the present moment is also about owning who you want to be in the future. It is about building your character and setting goals to develop, grow, and better yourself each day. It is about integrity, principles, and values. This means staying away from anyone or anything that tries to antagonize your character and the person you are striving to be.

Before making any decision, it is always important to ask yourself: "What am I hoping to achieve from this? What is my objective? What is my *intention*?" If the answer is anything from what you are trying to avoid or change about yourself, don't do it. Very simple.

If you know that you are a people-pleaser and you decide to do something that will do just that, then you are only going back to the thing you are trying your best to get away from. You are proactively *resisting* change.

It is extremely important to have a conversation with yourself—a healthy conversation—before you make any decision. Always question your thoughts and *challenge* them. Ask yourself why you are thinking a certain way. What triggered these thoughts? If you slept on it, would these thoughts remain? What would happen if you acted on these thoughts? How would it make you feel?

The Spotlight Effect has us thinking that people are paying more attention to us than they actually are. Instead of spending time focusing on how others see us, we need to clean the lens through which we see ourselves when we look in the mirror, and be a little kinder to ourselves. Remember, if you own every part of you, you no longer give anyone else the power to hold anything against you.

Rule 4:
Define What Success is to You

O nce you have shifted through the noise and zoomed out, you can begin to think clearly and apply Rule #4. Once you have understood how you think, identified your recurring thoughts and behavioral patterns, and found your way back to yourself, the next step is to respect your wants and needs and not society's. You need to define what success is to you, rather than what the world is telling you it is. This is the most important decision you will make at this specific moment in your life, because it will set the intention and direction for where you will go next.

Define what success or happiness is to you. It can be money, a healthy family, status, inner peace, or leaving the world a little better than you found it. Write it down, and revisit it. You will notice that your definition of success changes over time depending on which stage of your life you are in. Many people go through life not asking the simple question of what success means to them, and by the time they do, it is too late. For others, what they want out of life is crystal clear early on, and they live their entire lives pursuing that, and only that. There is no single version of success. Success has many shapes and forms and looks different to different people. You need to define what it looks like to *you*.

It doesn't have to make sense to others, but it has to make sense to you.

Success is different from goals. You can have goals along your journey to success. For people who suffer from depression, success can be getting out of bed every morning. For those who have social anxiety, success can be talking to a stranger or simply getting through the day. The big successes are not more important and should not be celebrated more than the small successes—because the small successes are actually the big ones.

If you are at school or university, success to you may be money. You are motivated—you want to pay off your school debt and are ready to make a life for yourself. Your goals, however (the tactics), can be getting into a good university, graduating with good grades, and landing a decent job. These are all steps along your journey to success.

You need to dig deep and continuously ask yourself why you want to achieve something. At first, you might think that success is getting into the corporate world. But that is not success—that is a goal. Ask yourself why you want to get into the corporate world—what is your objective?

If you have already landed your dream job and perhaps met someone along the way with whom you started a life, your definition of success might suddenly shift to wanting a healthy family and spending as much time with them as possible. What starts to happen is you begin to prioritize that. You can still have goals at work, but the objective or purpose of that goal is to provide a base for your family and perhaps health insurance in case they get sick. You will say no to after-work activities and want to come home to make it in time for dinner with your family before your kids go to sleep. Why? Because you have defined that that is what success is to you, and you are consciously and intentionally putting in the effort every day to not only reach it, but to maintain it once you have it.

Success looks different to different people. Being honest with yourself is key. Don't ever feel the need to want something because society makes you feel like you should want it. In a world that is trying to convince you that success is found in material possessions or relationships, you need to be strong enough not to fall for that. For me, making a warm cup of coffee in the morning, cleaning my house, going for a peaceful walk in nature, reading a book, or simply visiting my neighbors—that is *my* success. These things make *me* happy, not society. I do not do these things to post on social media that I did those things. People don't give a shit. They see it and then move on with their lives. They keep scrolling. So why should I place my happiness in their hands?

We all have to make a choice. A choice about what kind of life we want. And then, we have to say no to everything that isn't that. Life is all about decisions. The smallest, most insignificant decisions that shape who we are and the life we lead. The insignificant decisions that lead to the most significant outcomes.

Once we have identified what success means to us in this specific moment and determined the price for it, we have to be willing to let go of things we once held onto. We have to get rid of the dead weight in order to become lighter—only then will we have the ability to move on and grow. We have to have a strong character to be able to resist. To be able to say no. To be able to walk away. We must stay away from people who try to antagonize our character and everything we are trying to achieve. When we put standards for ourselves, we start making better and quicker decisions. This is easier said than done and takes a lot of work and self-love. It is a process, but once we start tasting how it feels, we can never go back.

If you are confused, you will send out confusing messages to the universe. You will notice that the people around you will be confused about what you want, and by trying to explain it to yourselves and them, you will end up confusing them more. Clarity is key. Paying attention to triggers is key. Asking yourself why it is you want or *think* you want something, is key. Challenge yourself, ask yourself questions, and have a conversation with yourself. You need to unravel the mystery that is your mind, and you need to understand it. You need to understand why you have the thoughts and beliefs that you do, and why you act the way that you do. Really take the time to get to know yourself. I know it's tough, and I know you will have to go places you would much rather not go to, but you need to be uncomfortable to make progress. The moment you speak of something and face it head on is the moment it no longer has power over you. Ask hard questions, and have the courage to be vulnerable. This world is a tricky place, and we need to be resilient. It is only getting tougher and tougher. The trick is simplicity. As the world is getting more complex, we need to go back to the basics and find peace and joy in the simple things.

What we want is often not in alignment with what is right for us. We need to learn to control those wants, in order to focus on what we need. Sometimes, the universe sends us everything we thought we wanted to show us that this is exactly not what we needed. Whatever and however you choose to live your life, the most important thing is to live it authentically.

Rule 5:

Leave the Past Where it Belongs

I f there is one thing I have learned in life, it is to never go back to your past. Yes, it is important to revisit your past in order to understand who you are today (and certainly who you are *not*), but that's it. It should only be used as a tool for reflection. Nothing more, nothing less. The past is in the past for a reason, and only fools trip on what is behind them.

We are all shaped by what has happened to us in our past—in our childhoods, relationships, and friendships. Regardless if those memories were good or bad, it is easy to keep living in the past. Part of the reason we hold on to it is because that is where our comfort zone lies. It is safe. We know the situation and the outcome. Sometimes we are too attached to the memories and feelings rather than the person or experience. When we find ourselves doing this, we need to remember two things:

1) Lots of things seem better in retrospect. This means we shouldn't trust our powers of recall because they're prone to errors.

2) *Peak-end rule:* we remember most clearly the peak of an incidence—i.e., the moment of greatest intensity—and the end. Barely anything else filters through into our memories.

We have complete power here:

We cannot change what happened in the past and how it made us feel at that moment, but we can choose how we respond to it. We can choose the story we tell ourselves.

We are not victims. Yes, we went through hard stuff, and it was a very shitty feeling. Yes, sometimes it still hurts when we are up late at night all alone and those thoughts take over. Yes, sometimes someone says something or we watch a movie or listen to a song, and all those memories and emotions start flooding right back. Yes, sometimes we remember and we cry. But we are not victims. We are survivors. We are *human*.

In fact, if someone were to ask you the question, "If you could go back in time and not experience those hard moments, would you?" The answer would probably be no. Because losing those experiences would also mean losing all the strength you gained from them.

We can be loyal to the moments and memories we shared with people, and still want to move on and have nothing to do with them.

We spend so much time and effort mourning the past and holding on to the history and memories we shared with people. We find ourselves doing this even more often if we are naturally loyal people. What we don't realize is that our relationships with people are temporary. Every single thing has an expiration date, including loyalty. This means that some people are only meant to come into your life to get you from point A to point B. That's it.

People are always going to be drawn to you for one reason or another. Similarly, we are drawn to certain people more than others for a reason. Every person we meet has something to teach us. Just like we have something to teach them. Trust that life has a natural way of filtering people from your life, and that will happen after that person has served their purpose.

Never choose loyalty over self-respect.

When someone lets go of you once, they will do it again. When someone shows you their true colors, believe them. Don't **ever** give people justifications or excuses for their actions, especially when they have given you every reason not to. Never chase after anyone. If they want to walk out of your life, guide them to the door. If they want you to step out of theirs, do so happily because, one day, they will be begging for you to ring the doorbell.

Never, ever make a decision to keep someone in your life based on history. We usually fear never finding someone who will make us feel those things again, no matter how toxic they are, and so we keep going back. That is completely normal. Remember, you should be focusing on who you need in your future and where you need to be. Going back to people from the past is a sign of weakness. Moving on takes strength and courage.

We all relapse. We all have moments of weakness where our thoughts overtake us, and we make spontaneous decisions that we later regret. However, the most important thing is not to be too hard on ourselves, and to allow ourselves to make those mistakes consciously. Being aware is what matters. Reflecting on those decisions afterward and asking ourselves questions to try to understand why we relapsed is extremely important. This will help us identify our triggers. Triggers are key. They are the root cause of all our behaviors. We need to identify them, acknowledge them, understand them, and make friends with them. Only then will they no longer have power over us. And only then will we be able to avoid moments of relapse as much as possible. We are creatures of habit. This means that once we identify a behavioral pattern that leads to those moments of relapse, we can change our habits and avoid future relapses.

Sometimes, it can be something as simple as hearing a line from a sad song. The song itself can bring back memories, or the words can trigger an emotional reaction. This causes us to start reminiscing and remembering the good times (remember the peak-end rule), which causes our thoughts to tell us that what we had was special, that the person was not as bad as we made them out to be, that maybe there's a chance we can work things out. So we give it one more shot. We go back. We relapse.

When someone has wronged you, the best thing you can give them is your silence. Being angry and upset will only harm you— forgiveness is the best gift you can give yourself. At the end of the day, the main focus should be on protecting yourself and your peace of mind—everything else will follow. Learn to know the difference between who deserves an explanation and who deserves absolutely nothing. Being vulnerable with the wrong person is not strength, it is weakness. Being silent with those who do not deserve our words is self-discipline and control. **There is strength in vulnerability. But there is also strength in silence.**

As Oprah said, "When we expect people to act like we would have acted in that specific situation, we get disappointed." Not everyone thinks like you. Not everyone has the same values as you. Not everyone has the same character as you. We need to understand that each person is different and deals with different situations differently. This does not mean that it is anything personal towards us, but it is their own internal struggles they are fighting with. Not all people know how to deal with confrontation. Not all people know how to verbalize their feelings. Not everyone knows how to be honest. A lot of people choose the easy way out—the *cowardly* way out. They lie, they cheat, and they run away. And that's okay. That is not our problem. It is not on us to fix them. It is on us to inspire them, to teach them, to love them, and to leave them a little better than we found them. That's it. The rest is up to them.

Don't ever give someone from your past enough power to dictate your future decisions. I've lost track of the times when I've seen people love hard, get their hearts broken, and say the words: "I'm done with relationships," "I'm done with men/women," or "I will never love again." Why are you allowing one single person to hold so much power over your life? If you had a shitty experience with a shitty person, that does not mean that all human beings are shitty. Shutting yourself off to the world because of one heartbreak is such a damn shame. Instead, learn from that experience. Ask yourself what that experience and what that person taught you about *yourself.* Hold yourself accountable. Ask yourself questions. Work on improving those things so you can be ready when the right person does come along.

Find peace in knowing that most people & things are temporary.

When you have experienced an emotional high so intense, you don't ever want to experience it again because it reminds you how hard the fall will be. Emotions do not belong to us—they are fleeting. And the moment we truly understand this concept, we start making better, more conscious decisions. It is easy to be drawn to things that make us feel because, after all, who are we really if we don't feel? The trick here is to link those feelings and emotions to a goal or a purpose—not to human beings. Especially if these human beings are not right for us. The person we love today can be gone tomorrow.

We need to understand the difference between loyalty and reality. We can be loyal to people and to the moments we've shared with them, but if reality kicks in and no longer provides us with the environment or comfort that allowed us to love and care for them, we have to let go. One thing is true: all things come to an end. It is up to us to let this happen naturally and not try to resist. Resistance will do things to your body and mind that will bring them off balance, and balance is key in everything you do and every single thought you have.

Every new chapter in your life will demand a new version of you.

Letting go is okay. In fact, it is incredibly liberating. It is okay to find yourself no longer enjoying the same conversations, people, and memories. It is okay to want to move on and start over.

If you find yourself being the smartest or wisest person in your group of friends, find new friends. If you find yourself in a different stage in your life, while others are in the same place, cut them loose—they are hindering your growth. Let go of the dead weight. Trust me; you will feel much lighter. If you never let go of old people, things, and places, you will never make room for new things to enter your life.

There is strength in solitude. There is strength in silence. There is strength in letting go.

PART II

Rule 6:

Always Trust Your Gut. Energy Never Lies

Always trust your gut. When something doesn't feel right, it probably isn't.

Have you ever walked into a room and felt like you could cut the tension with a knife? You could not really put your finger on it, but the air felt so thick, and there was just a wave of negativity. This exact feeling is felt when we meet certain people. They say and do all the right things, but for the life of us, *something just feels off.* Do you know this feeling? Trust it. That is your gut instinct telling you to be careful. That is your gut recognizing red flags before the logical part of your brain has even had time to process what is going on. The opposite holds true. With some people, there is an instant connection. Just their aura makes us feel good, and they have a positive energy or "vibe" that we are drawn to. They might not say much—they might not say anything at all—but we feel comfortable around them. We immediately know that we like them. This is not only applicable to individuals and groups, but to places, environments, and even animals. When you learn to trust yourself so much, you will find yourself making decisions based on intuition instead of logic. And believe me, intuition never lies.

Always pay attention to how the other person makes you feel. Even if that feeling is familiar, it does not mean it is right. If anyone, even for one second, makes you feel unworthy or less than, cut them out of your life without thinking twice. Learn to listen to your body; it will immediately tell you whether something is off. Over the years, my body has developed a defense mechanism where the warning signs and emergency bells immediately go off when something is not right, and I have become extremely good at reading and understanding these signs. Your gut has an extensive network of nerve cells and knows when something negative is being repeated before your brain even knows it. So, your body responds before the mind can comprehend what is going on. For me, this trigger or warning sign has been a lack of sleep. When something is bothering me and I cannot put my finger on it, I have trouble sleeping or suddenly wake up in the middle of the night. I used to think that something was wrong with me, but it was quite the opposite. I now know that I know what I want more than I think I do. It is that battle between my gut and mind that causes this disruption and confusion. The moments both of them are aligned are the moments I have clarity.

It is important to trust yourself enough to make decisions based on gut instinct. Make small commitments to yourself to build that trust. All of us have made poor decisions when it comes to relationships. We ignored our gut feelings and the red flags from the beginning and ended up wishing we could go back in time and trust ourselves more. After all, most relationships end due to the very same concern we had at the start, but chose to ignore.

With people, you can never really know where you stand, and feelings are up and down. That messiness, uncertainty, and instability are things you probably struggle with, just like everyone else. You have lost trust in your decisions because a lot of decisions you have made have been the wrong ones for you. As a result, you no longer trust your decision-making process and no longer have confidence in what you are doing. *Doubt* creeps in. However, if you look back on your relationships and what you learned from them, you will realize that you have, in fact, been right. You will realize that your only problem was not acting on your initial gut feeling—that 'whisper' from the start. Because that is exactly what it sounds like—a whisper. It is not loud, and it does not demand our attention. So, we often choose to ignore it.

The misalignment between your head and gut is a key metric in knowing whether the decisions you have made have been right or wrong for you. It is exactly how you know if you have still not found your person, if you are in the wrong job, or if you are surrounding yourself with the wrong group of people.

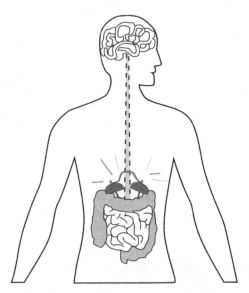

And then there is our ego. The ego is a dangerous thing. It silences the mind and controls the body. It is what keeps us going back to people and things that we know, without a shadow of a doubt, are not good for us. But it is hard to say no to the attention. It is hard to walk away from someone who made us feel so special, even if we didn't feel the same way. And so, we go back. We check their Instagram accounts one more time, send them that message, and keep that window just a tiny bit open in case they want to come back.

There is a fine line between ego and self-respect. Our ego is defensive. It is reactive. It cannot stand the thought of rejection. Our self-respect is quiet, calm and collected. It feels no need to provide explanations or convince anyone of anything—it simply knows when to walk away without a word.

The head and gut know it is okay to be rejected—in fact, it is extremely healthy. The head and gut know that how people act is nothing personal at all, and that every single person has their own trauma. The head and gut know that people will always come back because you arc a good soul, and good souls are extremely rare nowadays. The head and gut know that patience and time are two of your biggest assets, and that sometimes not doing or saying anything is the healthiest thing you can do. It is the ego that keeps getting in the way and tries to mess up the process and the journey.

The head and the gut are always crystal clear in what they tell us. Their voice is just not as loud as the ego, so we tend to ignore them. And this is what we need to change. We need to give them more self-love, nurture, and confidence so they can speak up. So they can overpower the ego. How do we do this? Through practicing stillness.

Now is the time to listen to the gut and the head again. It is time to start putting them first. It is time to forgive the ego for all the times it led you astray, and to apologize to our gut and mind for not listening to them sooner.

Rule 7:

Invest in Your Inner Peace

Why is it that all books, talks, articles, and lectures discuss return of investment (ROI) in financial terms? Why is everything centered around money all the time? I feel like people have been tricked. Tricked into believing that every single penny they invest and can bring them a financial return of investment is the ultimate goal. And so people start reading, listening, watching, and become obsessed with understanding the stock market and staying updated with recent trends so they can capture an opportunity, invest their money, and get a good return on that investment. Why haven't people stopped to think that the definition of

ROI extends far beyond money? Why haven't people asked themselves what the price of their inner peace is and how much of their investments are actually going into that? Why aren't people treating their time and energy as a currency and saving up on it as much as possible—just like they would with their money—and investing it in places, things, and people that will generate them an intangible, but more valuable return?

In Rule #4, we discussed the importance of defining what success is to you. Inner peace was one of those definitions of success. However, regardless of what we strive for in a specific chapter of our lives, we should always be mindful of our inner peace, and we should always invest in it. The level of investment might vary from person to person, but we should all actively do it regardless.

Inner peace comes from setting boundaries. From not allowing petty things to disrupt your mood and not allowing certain people and things to occupy a space in your mind that you could be using for something else. Inner peace comes from forgiving others and forgiving yourself. It is being intentional about what and who you give your time and energy to, and putting yourself above everyone else. It is about valuing yourself, nurturing yourself, caring for yourself, and loving yourself—without feeling guilty about it.

Most importantly, inner peace comes from acceptance. Accepting things for what they are and for what they will be. Not trying to force things, and certainly not trying to change them. Acceptance comes from knowing who you are—down to the very core—and being content with it. It is knowing that certain things are not within our control, and not living between the past and future. **Inner peace is when your values and beliefs are aligned with your actions.** When you can go to sleep at night knowing that you stayed true to who you are, and being proud of your character.

Investing in your inner peace means putting your needs first and finding ways to eliminate stress, anxiety, anger, resentment, and regret. It is about peace of mind and, ultimately, peace of body. When we treat our inner peace like a bank account, with energy and time as the currency, we become more mindful of how we spend it. We start being aware of places, things, and people that drain us, and we start to focus on saving as much as we can, just like we would with our money. Whether in the workplace or our personal lives, focusing on every detail that either drains us or fills us up is key. One thing that can help is keeping a journal. Write about what happened in your day and how it made you feel. Ask yourself why you felt extra tired after meeting up with a particular friend, or why you were energetic after your walk. Maybe that friend spent all of their time with you gossiping about others or complaining about their lives? Maybe listening about things that add no value to your life whatsoever drained you more than you realized? A walk in nature, on the other hand, spending time with yourself and admiring the beauty of the world around you, actually filled you up. Understanding how different things affect you will help you make wiser investment decisions and get a better ROI.

Learn to listen more and talk less.

Investing in your inner peace means protecting your energy. It is identifying things in your life that drain your energy and finding ways to control them. One thing that drains us more than we realize is talking and engaging in unnecessary conversations. With time, you learn to say less and listen more. You learn that not everything needs an explanation, and not everyone deserves a justification. You don't owe anyone anything. Absolutely nothing. No one knows your journey, and no one has been on your path. No one knows your struggles and what you went through to get to where you are today. Learning to listen not only allows you to pay attention to your surroundings and how you feel, but it also allows you to be in control of your reactions and be true to yourself.

Rule 8:
Find the Balance in Everything

E verything in life is about balance; whether it is religion, finances, raising kids, eating, spending, exercising, or working—it is all about balance. We need to know when to be lenient, when to be a little bit tougher, when to be harsh, when to forgive, and when to hold things in. Whenever we go into excess, something else must be destabilized. We need a middle path in everything.

"Everything in moderation."

– Oscar Wilde

In high school, they teach us early on about homeostasis and the internal balance of the body. This holds true in every single moment of our lives. We need to pay attention to how our external environment is regulating our internal environment, and we need to protect this balance with every cell in our body. When there is balance, there is harmony. Everything is where it is supposed to be. You can feel it on the inside and the outside. When things are not where they are supposed to be, you are disturbed.

Throughout this book, we have mentioned balance several times, and you will notice that it is a crucial concept in our journey to finding clarity.

Clarity cannot be achieved without balance.

The first step is identifying the external factors that are throwing you off balance. Remember, in Rule #1, we discussed the importance of balance in social media and technology. We mentioned that it is necessary to turn down the volume to focus on what is truly important. In a digitalized world, balancing between time spent staring at a screen and the time spent physically connecting with those around you is crucial. In order to do this, we need to be disciplined. We also mentioned practical steps that could be taken, including putting your phone on airplane mode, keeping it in a different room when you sleep, or leaving it at home when you go for walks. All of these actions will allow you to minimize the effects of dopamine and allow you to think clearly.

Work-life balance

Another external factor is our work and the distractions that come with it. Know when to turn off your phone, email notifications, laptop, and, most importantly, your mind. Find that balance between disconnecting from work and connecting with family and yourself.

Most of us are built to interact—we are gregarious by nature. We need people around us, and we need to have relationships. Sitting in an office or working from home will not allow us to have that. In the world we live in today, ordering food with the press of a button and taking meetings on Zoom or Teams limits our physical interaction with other humans and leaves us feeling distressed. Unless this is compensated in other ways to satisfy our need for that interaction, we end up with more anxiety, stress, and depression.

If you are unhappy at your job, the solution is not always to quit because life is not that simple. We all have mortgages to pay, mouths to feed, and responsibilities to fulfill. However, what we can do is manage our time in order to be more content. We can say no to unnecessary meetings, turn off our phones after working hours, wake up an hour earlier to read or meditate, or take up a hobby. We can recognize that we are unhappy at a job but still be grateful that we even have one. We can stop complaining, stop victimizing ourselves, and see that job as something essential that we need to do in order to be able to do things we *want* to do.

Examples of balance:

- Knowing when to use technology and social media and when to avoid it.
- Working hard and spending time with family.
- Socializing (with positive people) and spending time alone.
- Being ambitious and focused, but also taking the time to enjoy life and relax.
- Earning money and making the time to spend it.
- Knowing when to stay and when to walk away.

Look for symptoms that you are off balance. One of those symptoms is negative mood. Notice how your body feels after using social media, reading the news, or spending time with certain people (we mentioned this in previous chapters). If your mood is lower and your energy is drained, then something is off balance.

Another very important symptom is declining health.

Your health has a tremendous effect on your quality of life. Finding that balance of enough sleep, a healthy diet, and physical activity is crucial to living a peaceful and productive life. Your body is the most reliable indicator of when things are out of control. One of those signs is poor sleep quality. For others, it can be a lack of appetite or gastrointestinal problems. It can also be physical pain, headaches, or overall irritability. Remember, either too much, or too little of anything can harm you. Sleeping too much is not good for your health, and sleeping too little isn't either. Drinking too little water is unhealthy, and drinking too much water can be dangerous.

Once you have identified the external factors that are throwing you off balance, you need to determine which internal factors are preventing you from achieving that balance (remember to live from the inside out). Your core beliefs might make it difficult to build new, positive habits that allow you to be disciplined, and you might find yourself going back to people and things that are not good for you and that throw you off balance. This is why it is essential to work on understanding yourself, so you can understand what is holding you back (Rule #2). Once you understand that, you can take small steps to work towards your goal. It is a process that takes time—but you will get there.

Negative self-worth, bad habits, and toxic behavioral patterns are all symptoms that something is off balance.

Children need discipline. They appreciate discipline. They need to eat and sleep at a specific time each day, and there must be a strict schedule. If there isn't, the child will be cranky and in a bad mood, with no structure to their life. The same holds true for adults.

Finding and maintaining balance in your life requires self-discipline. Without self-discipline, you end up wasting time, procrastinating, and not following through on important tasks. Balance is about implementing positive life habits and staying disciplined throughout the process. Building those habits takes time, so we must remember to be patient with ourselves.

Counterproductivity

If we look around us, everything is trying to throw us off balance. It is draining our energy and making us lose focus. And we are falling right into the trap. We are overcomplicating things way more than we should. At work, there are too many unnecessary meetings where the entire team is invited to discuss a topic that could easily be addressed and concluded between two individuals in five minutes over the phone. There are way too many communication channels, like Teams, Zoom, and Trello, where just simply sending an email gets the point across. We spend hours scrolling through endless options on Netflix only to fall asleep without choosing anything, or go back to an old movie or series just to feel like we watched something. We use our phones to take over fifteen photos doing the exact same pose, then spend hours editing them or deciding what to post and what to delete. Back in the day, we had a specific number of clicks on the camera in a "film," and we guarded those clicks with our lives. The photos that we did take, we kept for years and years because they had value, and the poses we struck in those pictures were so natural and spontaneous. They were *authentic*. Now we keep thousands of photos in our camera roll, then struggle to find them or forget that we even have them because they have ended up on iCloud or mysteriously disappeared when we decided to change phones. Everything we do is counterproductive. Technology is advancing, but we are moving *backward*.

Those of us who experienced the "simple days" would probably give anything to go back. The over-complication of today's world is why we crave the basics. It is the reason why people leave big corporate companies to join start-ups. It is why people still prefer to use flipcharts over PowerPoint, and why many people still choose to buy hardcover books instead of e-books.

When it comes to relationships and modern dating, the abundance of dating apps and "swiping" features has created too many options and confusion. Before the era of technology and social media, we had limited options, and this meant that we put more effort into the choices we did have in order to make them work. Today, we can swipe through on thousands of different profiles on dating apps—and so we believe we have endless options. Because of this, there is less value and satisfaction in the choices we make. Not only are we confused by the options, but we are also wasting our time and energy.

Finding balance and clarity in a world of technology comes from learning to simplify our lives again, no matter how challenging it is. This can include buying an actual alarm clock as opposed to using our phones, listening to the radio through an actual radio, training ourselves to click only once when we take a photo on our phones, learning to live in the present and enjoy a moment without feeling the need to post about it, and saying no to unnecessary meetings and complex platforms.

We are creatures of habit. And the more we train ourselves to do these very simple things, the more we will notice that it will become our new normal.

We cannot change the direction of the world and where it is headed, but we can decide how we respond to it and how we allow those changes to affect us.

Balance cannot be achieved without self-discipline and self-awareness. This includes knowing how and where to invest our energy (Rule #7). By identifying where our energy is currently being placed, we can intentionally redirect and reinvest it, and get one step closer to achieving balance and clarity.

Rule 9:

Search for Compatibility &
Respect. Love is Overrated

Anyone who has experienced love and gotten hurt has probably sworn that they will never love again. But that's a lie. It is the feeling of pain that we have sworn we never want to feel again, but the feeling of love is something we will always crave. As humans, we want to feel. And we want to feel things deeply. Even if that means it comes with the risk of getting hurt. However, as we grow older and have more experiences, we tend to become a little more closed off unconsciously. Our hope of a fairy tale slowly diminishes, and what ends up happening for some of us is we start to settle. For others, the more they see and experience, the more they realize what they want and do not want in a partner, and the higher their standards become. There are also those whose fear of rejection becomes stronger than their need for love, and they completely sabotage any potential connections. Then there are those who have gone through such bad experiences that they have nothing more to give or no longer know how to feel. In all cases, the result is the same. People either end up in unhappy relationships or end up alone.

If you ask someone what love is, you would notice that each person's definition of love is different depending on their experience.

Human beings are narcissistic by nature. This degree varies from individual to individual. This means that when we "love" someone, we don't actually love them for who they are, but for how they make *us* feel. If you ask someone why they love their partner, most of the time, they will say, "I love how they take care of me,"

"I love the way they love me," or "I love how safe they make me feel." It usually has very little to do with the actual person, and more with what that person offers us, and how they make us feel about ourselves. They are either complementing us by filling a gap that we have, or nurturing our inner child. It is important to note here that how they make us feel about ourselves is not necessarily a good feeling; it can also be a *familiar* feeling. This is why people stay in toxic relationships or keep going back to someone who treated them poorly. It is because, despite how shitty they make them feel, they somehow like it. It is something familiar due to past trauma, and for some reason, they enjoy that feeling. Getting treated well is too boring for some people.

For these reasons, you need to pay very close attention to toxic people in your life. People you have cut off but keep showing up in your life whenever they please. An ex who hurt you and suddenly decided to reach out does not miss you. Do not feel special. They are just looking for a temporary ego boost to know they still have power over you. It is **not** to get back with you. They are motivated by the challenge, not by the outcome. In fact, them showing up in your life after you have tried to move on is the most selfish thing anyone can do. But the feeling of no longer being chased and pursued by you is too hard for their ego. So they pop back into your life to remind you that they're still there, and to get you to start thinking about them again.

Attachment styles

The moment that changed everything for me was when I got introduced to attachment styles. This was a breakthrough moment that not only helped me identify a pattern in my past relationships, but also helped me understand myself so much better and the reason why I was attracting and was attracted to certain people. Just like in the stock market, there are trends in our lives. Patterns. We just have to pay close attention. And despite the messiness of the world, there is structure amid this chaos.

According to psychiatrist and neuroscientist Dr. Levine, there are categories for our behavior. These are known as attachment styles and primarily consist of:

- Secure
- Anxious
- Avoidant

Without going into too much detail, we develop different attachment styles as kids to help us survive in a given environment. Your attachment with your caretaker as a child plays a role in the attachment you will form with your partner. People who are distant, inconsistent in their behavior, and have a difficult time committing and trusting others are usually **avoidant**. These are the ones who had to self-soothe as children, and learned to rely on themselves early on. Those who had a secure love where if they felt hurt, they could go to a place for safety and would be embraced and cared for would most probably have a **secure** attachment style as adults. **Anxious** attachment is seen in individuals whose parents worked most of the time and could not necessarily be there when the child needed them, making the child anxious about their love. As adults, this is manifested as being "needy."

Love looks different to different people. But is it enough?

Love on its own is an unreliable concept. You can love someone deeply, but that is not enough to make a relationship work. Love comes and goes, and can fade over time. What remains is the way you treat each other. You can love someone but not like them. A relationship often ends the same way it began.

When you first meet someone, there are always signs. Red flags. Gut instinct. Your intuition knows someone long before your brain has had time to process their character. But the mistake here is that we disregard our gut because the image our brain has drawn for us is way more attractive and appealing. It matches society's expectations of us, so the first thing we want to do is jump to the part where we can tell the world we are taken and start picturing the white picketed fence.

Do not search for love. Instead, search for compatibility, consistency, and respect. The first thing that you should notice right off the bat is the person's energy and how they make you feel. *How do they make your nervous system feel?* Do you leave them feeling drained or energized? Do you leave them knowing exactly where you stand, or are you confused? Second, pay attention to that person's behavior. They can make you feel good in the moment, but are they consistent? Do their words and actions match? Do they clearly communicate their feelings, and are they open about emotions and deep topics? This part is crucial because it gives you an indication of the person's attachment style. Finally, do their values align with yours? How do they treat the waiter at a restaurant? Do they act with integrity? Most importantly, do they respect you?

According to a matchmaker, Paul Brunson, there is a specific blueprint you can follow to determine if you are compatible with someone. This includes attachment styles, which we previously mentioned, similar values, and the ability to communicate, which consists of the ability to make collaborative decisions together. Finally, physical attraction is crucial. If you have minimal physical attraction, that can build and grow over time. However, if you have zero physical attraction from the start, chances are, it will not work out. A key factor here is respect—that should be the red thread. Respect and compatibility can lead to love over time, but love does not always equate to respect and compatibility.

When we are overpowered by emotions, we tend not to think clearly.

Letting go of the belief that love should feel a certain way with emotional highs and lows will save us from a lot of unrealistic expectations. With time, we start not to want to feel those highs because they cloud our judgment. We begin to realize the difference between lust and love, physical and soul attraction, and clarity and confusion. We start to search for that feeling of calmness rather than "weak at the knees." We look to be calm in love, not crazy in love.

Focusing on the key metrics—the blueprint—will allow us to make wiser decisions, not only for ourselves, but for those around us. If you are looking for a romantic relationship, you need to put in the work towards yourself. You need to work on enhancing your communication, emotional intimacy, listening skills, and, most importantly, self-awareness. These will not only help you in your romantic life, but in all aspects of your life. If you are in a relationship and you are unhappy, you need to ask yourself these fundamental questions. The main one being—is there respect, and are you compatible (regardless of how much you love them)? If the answer is no—is there work you can do individually and as a couple to fix this? One option is to try couples therapy or individual therapy. Therapy is not a quick fix and will definitely not solve all of your problems, but it will help you start building that muscle. It will then be your responsibility to continue that process. Anything that you are interested in requires you to put in the effort. There may be nothing that can be fixed—you will just need to accept that, close that chapter, and move on.

Based on my own experiences and learnings, here are some of my main takeaways about love and relationships:

- Stay away from someone whose love for their ego is bigger than their love for you.

- Be with a great communicator.

- Just because someone treated you well, it does not mean they're the one.

- A lot of people can buy you material things, but not everyone can understand your silence.

- Look for consistency, and always pay attention if the person's actions match their words.

- Always notice how that person makes you feel about yourself. Notice the words they use with you—do they put you down or lift you up?

- Be with someone who constantly reassures you, not gets annoyed with you.

- Choose someone who is thoughtful, values you, and takes even your smallest needs seriously.

- Look for someone who doesn't just apologize with words but through changed behavior.

- If something didn't work out the first time, there's a high probability it never will.

- Never chase after anyone. If they want to walk out of your life, guide them to the door. If they want you to step out of theirs, do so happily because, one day, they will beg you to ring the doorbell.

- Know your worth. Stay away from people who make you feel less than.

- What comes quickly, goes quickly ("Easy come, easy go").

Rule 10:

Never Give Yourself Permission to Judge Anyone. Always Humble Yourself

Take a minute to appreciate this moment right here and now. Close your eyes. Breathe. You will never be who you are after this specific moment, and who you are now is different from who you were before this moment arrived. Everything that has happened in your life up until this moment has shaped you into the person you are now. This second. You should be so proud of yourself and how far you have come.

We tend to forget just how blessed we are. We were born in a specific country, into a specific postcode, and into a specific family. Yes, there are decisions that our parents and generations before them made that led them to where they are today, such as their choice of spouse, but a lot of it is luck too. A friend of mine once told me, "My kids cannot choose their parents, but I can choose their mother." And that hit deep. Those of us born into a wealthy or middle-class society could have easily been born in a third-world country. The basic needs we take for granted today are things people only dream of having. Access to clean water, electricity, and a sewage system—these are all things that we rarely even think about because they are just there. So, instead of seeing this as a gift, we see it as a given right. This is why traveling is so crucial. Experiencing different cultures—*really* experiencing them, not just traveling to a place, staying at a five-star hotel and going to tourist attractions just to post them on social media— is so vital for our minds. We need to interact with locals, see how they live, be curious, and ask questions. Only then will we open our minds to what other people in different parts of the world are going through. Only then will we truly have an appreciation for what we have. If we cannot afford to travel or have specific circumstances that make it difficult to, we need to find ways to meet people from different cultures and ask questions. This can be your next-door neighbor, colleague at work, or someone you meet at a café. Or it can simply be reading a book. Be curious. Don't judge. Have an open mind.

It is extremely easy in the world we live in to judge people based on how they look, the way they dress, their skin color, ethnicity, or even their political views. We tend to form a judgment about someone in the first few seconds of meeting them. In fact, it is very interesting when we look at the role politics has had in dating over the years. Just two decades ago, politics was insignificant in relationships, and it did not really matter if the person you were seeing had an opposing political view.

Today, it is one of the top metrics for whether or not you want to pursue someone romantically. Numerous studies have shown that a significant percentage of both men and women refuse to be physically intimate with someone with opposing political beliefs, regardless of how physically attracted they are to them. Nowadays, we are so quick to form judgments about the person, not based on *who* they are, but on *what* they believe in.

I remember walking with my boss and our colleague to have lunch. My boss—a tall, handsome Scandinavian—was telling us about a podcast he heard. He told us that the girl on the podcast was sharing how she would save up most of her money and was living on a tight food budget. He then went on to say, "Saving is good, but it is important to live your life as well and not be too stingy." This clearly offended my colleague. She looked at him and said, "M, you are very privileged in Sweden. The government provides everything for you. For a lot of people, this is not the case. They are struggling to meet their basic needs." As someone who had experienced struggle, left her friends and family in China and moved to Sweden to create a better life for herself and them, this clearly triggered her. My boss was taken aback by this but immediately realized that what he said may have come across as self-entitled. So, he replied, "You are right, my mistake."

Never ever give yourself permission to judge another human being. You don't know what they are going through. Also, be very mindful about the words you choose to say and the blessings you share with those who come from a different background than you.

As we grow older, we begin to understand the struggles of those around us. It makes us realize that the world is not as perfect as it seems. Every single one of us has trauma, trigger points, and voids, and every single person has a story. Just because some pain is obvious, that does not take away from the pain that is silent. Do not expect people to understand you. Instead, work on learning to understand others. Only then will you learn to take nothing personally.

Rule 11:

What You Try to Control, Will End Up Controlling You

O ne thing we cannot control is what people say and how they think or feel. Only they can do that. That is why relationships can be so tricky. We can control our own words, but we cannot control *how* people will feel about those words. Certain words and topics might be triggers, and that is something we can never know when we say them, no matter how mindful we are. Equally, we cannot control what people say to us and how they say it. What we *can* control, however, is how we respond to it.

> *"I am in control of my actions—I am not in control of your thoughts."*
>
> *- K.F*

The more we try to control how others view us, how they love us, and how they talk to us, the more we are being controlled. We are giving power to the very people we are seeking power from.

Anything that you give your energy to grows. If you focus on controlling your money to the point where you calculate every penny you spend, money will end up controlling you. If you try to control your physical appearance and photo edits in order to control the number of likes you get on Instagram, your insecurities will control you. If you focus on controlling the future by worrying about every worst-case scenario, stress will control you. Planning is healthy, but worrying is stressful. Nothing should occupy a space in our thoughts for too long. If it is, and those thoughts start dictating our everyday decisions and actions, they are controlling us.

The moment we breathe, let go, and let life happen the way it should, is the moment we are truly in control. Life has a way of mocking us and throwing us curveballs every now and then. Just when we think we have planned every possible scenario or outcome in our heads—life happens. Something so unexpected suddenly occurs that leaves us feeling silly for wasting our time and energy on something so unnecessary.

Anyone who has experienced grief knows what I'm talking about. Anyone who has experienced the loss of a loved one or knows someone who passed away unexpectedly knows that we could have never prepared for it. Grief is normal. It hurts, and it sucks. And we need to normalize talking about it without being afraid to make others uncomfortable.

Trying to control every single detail of our lives is tiring. In fact, it is exhausting. We need to learn to just be. To ride the wave of life and not be afraid to fall and get back up. We should not take ourselves and those around us too seriously. We tend to complicate things in our heads when, in reality, things are much simpler than we think. We need to have faith and trust that when something difficult happens— because life will happen—we will be prepared to deal with it. We will deal with it when it comes. Until then, there is no point stressing or worrying because the thing you are stressing about will probably never happen. Something else will instead, and you will have wasted your time and energy over nothing.

Rule 12:

There is Something Bigger Than You

R ules are healthy. They provide us with structure and guidance. They discipline us. However, all of us know that all rules have exceptions. All of us have experienced things ourselves or through others that have not made sense—things that could not be explained. Things that were out of our control. Regardless of how well we think we know what we want out of life and how hard we work towards a certain goal, sometimes life happens and makes us rethink our path and our priorities. This can include the death of a loved one, a sudden illness, an accident, or a global incident such as an earthquake, a hurricane, a tsunami, or even a pandemic. All of these occurrences are not within our control, and we always have to keep this in the back of our minds in everything we do. No matter how much we think we are in control of our lives, something greater than us is calling the shots. Whether you believe in God, the Universe, karma, or a Higher Power, you need to believe that there is something bigger than you and me.

For me, my faith has played a tremendous role in my journey of peace and clarity. It grounds me, humbles me, and gives me the strength to trust and let go. We need to take a step back every once in a while and zoom out. We need to see the bigger picture, even if what we are zooming out into is something that we cannot see. We are on this Earth for a reason; each one of us has a purpose, and we can never know what tomorrow has in store for us. We need to trust the process, and trust that it will all work out. We need to trust and believe that life is not happening *to* us; it is happening *for* us. Every hardship is meant to teach us something. All we need to do is listen. We need to pay attention and change course when needed.

We need to remember not to take things too seriously and to always laugh in stressful situations. If it won't matter in five weeks, it is not worth stressing over.

As humans, we always want to be around what makes us comfortable—whether it is other human beings, a home, or an object. We tend to easily become attached to what lies in our comfort zone, and the moment we lose it, we become terrified and do not know how to cope without it. A void must be filled immediately; unless something better comes along, we will constantly dwell on the past. However, humans tend to forget that we are adaptive organisms, and we will adapt no matter the situation. We must. That's the beautiful thing about how we were created. It is why people who lose their loved ones move on sooner or later—because if they didn't, life would stop for them. And life does not stop for anyone, whether we like it or not. That's how my grandmother coped with the loss of my grandfather after over sixty years of marriage. He was all she had and all she lived for. But life had to go on. She had to stay strong for her daughters and her family because if she fell apart, so would everyone else. And let's not forget how big of a role her faith played in her coping mechanism; her belief was so strong that it acted as her comfort and source of strength, and that eased the pain. That is something beautiful, in my opinion—having something you believe in so strongly that it acts as a justification for all the evil and good in this world. Some might even say that, without faith, you are as lost as a human soul can be. Once you believe that everything truly happens for a reason, and you learn to trust God and let go, you will see the world from a whole new perspective.

This life is an illusion. We all get so caught up in it, we don't even realize how fleeting it is. In one single moment, everything can be taken away from us. Just like that. Our time on Earth is limited. This is the most freeing thing ever. Instead of worrying about the future, focus on the now. Focus on making a difference in people's lives. On being a good person. The next time your food arrives at a restaurant, instead of pausing to take a photo, pause to thank God for the blessings He has bestowed upon you.

When we die, people do not remember what we owned, what our title was, or how wealthy we were. They remember if we were a good person. They remember how we made them smile, how we offered them a snack when they were hungry, and how we were always kind to them. These are the things that people remember. Character.

Do not let little things take up so much of your time and energy. Let go. What's meant to be will be. Whoever does not like you has always disliked you, and that will never change, no matter how hard you try. And people who genuinely love you and cherish you will always see the good in you no matter how badly you hurt them. So, stop trying so hard for people who are not worth your time and energy. Focus on the good, and good will continue to follow you. Focus on the negativity while surrounding yourself with negative people, and you will never lead a positive life.

References:

1. Woods, H.C. and Scott, H. (2016), #Sleepyteens: Social media use in adolescence is associated with poor sleep quality, anxiety, depression and low self-esteem. Journal of Adolescence, 51: 41-49. https://doi.org/10.1016/j.adolescence.2016.05.008

2. Eddins, R. (2022, May 10). *Uncover your core beliefs so you can change them.* Eddins Counseling Group – Houston & Sugar Land, TX. Retrieved January 9, 2023, from https://eddinscounseling.com/uncover-core-beliefs-can-change/

3. Hodge, R. (2020, February 25). *60% of people worry that Tech is moving too fast, study finds.* CNET. Retrieved October 15, 2022, from https://www.cnet.com/tech/tech-industry/global-trust-in-technology-declining-report-says/

4. Levine, A., & Heller, R. (2019). *Attached: Are you anxious, avoidant or secure? How the science of adult attachment can help you find - and keep - love.* Bluebird.

5. *What is globalization?* PIIE. (2022, October 24). Retrieved December 9, 2022, from https://www.piie.com/microsites/globalization/what-is-globalization

6. Winn, D. M. (2022, June 1). *How childhood beliefs are formed and why they matter.* Author Don Winn's Blog. Retrieved December 9, 2022, from https://donwinn.blog/2022/02/08/how-childhood-beliefs-are-formed-and-why-they-matter/

Printed in Great Britain
by Amazon